Beatrice Is Brown

Written by Darcy Carrillo

Illustrated by Hafsa Pinar

This Book Belongs To

____

To little Darcy.

Beatrice is brown.

She has skin like the moth's wing,

And eyes like two bears trudging
along the snow.

Her hair is black like the crow.

Bharat is brown.

His skin is as brown as tiger's eye.

His hair is as soft and black as the dahlia's petals.

His eyes are like two seeds, waiting
to sprout once the rain settles.

Benjamin is brown.

He has skin kissed by the sun,

And eyes like two elderberries,
destined to heal.

His hair is black like the
panther that stalks his meal.

Brisa is brown.

Her skin is like nutmeg and cinnamon.

Her eyes are like two dollops of
maple syrup on a plate of porcelain.

Her hair is brown like the leaves
that fall in autumn.

Brown is

beautiful!